Praise for *21 W*
Non-Fiction B

"Kristen gives a spectacular presen.... really motivates you to reach for the next level, and she can help you find that 'extra something' you need to complete your project. She truly is *The Ultimate Book Coach*."

—Michelle Lucas, Life Coach

"If you've got a manuscript idea in your head that is trying to get out, you'll want to read this inspirational little book. Short on pages but big on ideas, *21 Ways to Write & Publish Your Non-Fiction Book* gives you practical solutions for turning your brainchild into a published book faster and easier than you would have thought possible."

—Sue Collier, co-author of *The Complete Guide to Self-Publishing, 5th Edition*, and *Jump Start Your Books Sales, 2nd Edition*; and blogger at www.SelfPublishingResources.com

"If you're not connected with Kristen, you're totally missing out."

—Kelli Smith Claypool, Unconventional Business Coach

"No fluff, just the good stuff. With a little chocolate sauce added, of course, because that's Kristen's one weakness ...but at least she's consistent. Whether you are aching to write a book, sorta think you might want to write a book, or have been advised that you must write a book for some business credibility reason, be sure to start with Kristen's *21 Ways to Write & Publish Your Non-Fiction Book*. You're sure to save time, energy, and money if you heed her experienced, knowledgeable advice. Great job and I can't wait to recommend this to the myriad of folks I run into who say, "Hey, I've been thinking about writing a book, what should I do?" My answer now will be easier... "Dude (or dudette), get Kristen Eckstein's little book, read it twice, and then if you still want to write a book, go for it!""

—Bruce Brown, co-author of the *31 Days to Mastery* series

"Kristen is my go-to source on anything publishing. She's wise beyond her years and all of the courses and books she's written that I've gone through are outstanding and worth every penny."

—Erica Cosminsky, author of *The Invisible Office*

"Kristen is my personal rockstar. I love her energy, encouragement, and expertise when it comes to the world of book publishing. It's because of her passion for promoting others through books that I'm moving forward with not one, but *two* books! I'm thrilled and honored to call Kristen my book coach."

—Maruxa Murphy, Branding Strategist, InstantExpertBranding.com

"Kristen is a joy to work with and is so inspiring! She is also very knowledgeable about writing and the publishing industry. If you are looking for a professional to help you publish your next book, you'll enjoy working with Kristen."

—Rhea Perry, EducatingForSuccess.com

"Kristen Eckstein was a tremendous support to me as I went through the process of publishing my book. She is extremely knowledgeable about anything to do with book publishing and perhaps *the* best book cover designer in the industry."

—D'vorah Lansky, M.Ed. and author of *Connect, Communicate, and Profit*, www.ConnectCommunicateProfit.com"

"I've always loved to write and believe it's a true gift. However, never in my wildest dreams did I imagine writing a book, much less two! With Kristen's guidance and easy tips, I was able to independently publish my first book, then I was contacted by a traditional publisher for my next. Thanks Kristen!"

—Dr. Daisy Sutherland, Founder/CEO of Dr. Mommy Online, author of *Dr. Mommy's Life Lessons*

21 Ways to
Write & Publish Your
Non-Fiction Book

21 WAYS

to **write** &
publish your
non-fiction **book**

Kristen Eckstein

Discover! BOOKS™
an Imprint of Imagine! Books™

High Point, North Carolina

21 Ways™ Series, Book 1

Published by Discover! Books™
an Imprint of Imagine! Books™
PO Box 16268, High Point, NC 27261
contact@artsimagine.com

Imagine! Books™ is an enterprise of Imagine! Studios™
Visit us online at www.artsimagine.com

ISBN 13: 978-0-9767913-7-9
Library of Congress Control Number: 2011923958

First Discover! Books™ printing, March 2011

Dedication

For all those who have picked up a pen and
wondered what to write. You inspire me.

Acknowledgements

My eternal thanks goes to:

My Writing fan page audience at
Facebook.com/WritingFan—your comments,
ponderings and challenges inspired this book.

My editor, Erin Casey, for all your hard work
making the text (and me) look great.

My husband and guru book designer, Joe
Eckstein, for making the design of this book
stand out from the crowd.

Sue Collier, Felicia Slattery, Phil Simon and
Yolanda Johnson-Bryant for being brave
enough to review and endorse this little book.

And to all the aspiring authors in the past,
present and future who have given me the
honor of "sucking" the book out of their heads
and getting it into print. You fuel my passion.

Introduction

The first half of this little book tackles various ways to get your book out of your head and onto paper. Writing a book is not easy, but it is extremely rewarding. Every author I interview says they thought writing was the hardest part of creating a book—until they started the publishing process. Thus, the second half of this book deals with publishing and the various forms it can take. My hope is that you'll use the ideas and information here to write and publish your book quickly and easily. Above all, I hope it helps you find the writing and publishing options that suit you best.

Happy Writing!

Part 1

Ways to Get Your Book Written

Compile Articles

If you are writing non-fiction, segmenting your knowledge into manageable pieces (a.k.a. articles or blog posts) is one of the best ways to get started. Articles and blog posts are excellent tools, not only to use in promoting yourself and your future book, but also for creating and organizing material.

Here are five steps to write a book using a compilation of articles:

Step 1

Write down a broad topic or area of expertise in which you are well-versed. It can be something you have taught in a workshop, information related to your occupation, or something people frequently ask you about.

Step 2

Make an outline of twelve to sixteen specific things people should know about that topic. Start by listing questions you are commonly asked by followers, friends, and at live events. Your answers to these questions can be the different points on your outline.

Step 3

Choose one item on your outline and write at least four or five paragraphs about it. Write an introduction to the concept, some how-to or step-by-step points (such as this entry in this book), or general tips about that item.

Step 4

You will likely come across a few points that you need to research further. Don't stop writing to jump immediately into fact finding. Instead, use the comment tool in Microsoft Word to make a note of what you need to research. You can change the color of the text in question to make it easy to find that section in the future.

Or, insert three asterisks (like this: ***) to mark a section that needs additional information. Then you can do a Find -> Replace in your word processing program to easily locate these areas. Remember, *don't pause your progress to research the topic.* Maintain your momentum and handle all the research once the writing is complete.

Step 5

Once you have written anywhere from a few paragraphs to a few pages for each item on your outline, organize the articles in the order that makes the most sense to you. Read your newly compiled manuscript from start to finish. Congratulations! You have written a book!

2

Ghostwritten

Some people find that it is easy to develop an outline, but difficult to write the actual material. Don't let this be a stumbling block! Ghostwriters can take your outline, complete all the detailed research, and handle the task of writing. Most celebrity and political books are written by ghostwriters.

However, you do not have to hire a ghostwriter to write your entire book for you. There are several ways you can work with a ghostwriter.

Outline

Create an outline with several sub-points and send it to a ghostwriter who specializes in writing complete books.

Articles

Provide your ghostwriter with a collection of articles you have written. Stringing articles together can potentially result in a disjointed mess that doesn't make much sense as a book to the reader. A ghostwriter can cross-reference the material, add transitions, and create a book that flows logically from one article (chapter) to the next.

Teleseminars

If you have transcriptions from teleseminars, give them to a ghostwriter as content for your book. An hour's worth of audio yields about thirty pages of text. A good ghostwriter can smooth the flow of speech into a format that is easy and natural to read while maintaining your unique style.

The option of having a book ghostwritten is ideal for busy businesspeople or speakers who have three or four core presentations that they wish to compile into one book for back-of-the-room sales.

WAY **3**

Interview Style

If you have an online business, consider interviewing other people in your industry and niche. Have them sign an agreement that allows you to repurpose the interview in any way you please. Most people are agreeable to this arrangement because it offers them additional, free publicity.

Hire a transcriptionist who specializes in transcribing for the purpose of books. I recommend *The Small Business Transcriptionist* (TheSmallBusinessTranscriptionist.com). Expect to wait twenty-four to forty-eight hours for the transcriptions to be returned, depending on the service you use.

Once you receive the transcriptions, send them to a ghostwriter (see "Way 2") or developmental editor to divide up into chapters, headings, subheadings, and make the content flow. You can choose to either keep it interview style (less time), or develop the text so it flows as a complete chapter without question and answer headings.

After you get the transcribed interviews back from the ghostwriter or editor, put the manuscript into publication—you have a book!

Host a Teleseminar

One of the best ways to get content for a book quickly is to host a teleseminar or telesummit. A telesummit usually involves other people and can either be conducted interview style or the guest expert can strictly teach content. A teleseminar is either a class taught by you, or a single class that is part of a larger telesummit.

If you host a series of teleseminars or teach several different teleseminars on the same general topic, you can get the recorded audios transcribed into text (see "Way 3" for my recommended transcription service).

It is important to use either a ghostwriter or developmental editor when creating a book from transcribed teleseminars. We don't speak the way we read, so spoken content must be significantly reworked. Using transcripts can be one of the fastest ways to create a book, but it will be more expensive than straight writing.

5

Go on a Retreat

Sometimes a few days away from life and all its distractions can work wonders on our writing lives. I personally try to take a writing retreat once each year.

In 2009, I spent ten days at the beach and wrote for three-and-a-half of those days. During that time, I was able to get all the content out of my head and onto paper for my book, *Financial Revival: A Lifestyle of Freedom*. (Visit WriteMyBookIn3Days.com for a free webinar on the strategies I used to get this 180-page book out of my head and onto paper so quickly.)

In 2010, I found a group that specializes in writers' retreats: My Writer's Connection (MyWritersConnection.com). I attended the group's retreat/cruise. During our two full days at sea and in between workshops, I nailed down six chapters for one of my next books, *What You Need2Know About: Publishing*.

Because that retreat included workshops, I also gained insight into my writing career from other professionals in the field. We received feedback on the assignments and learned a lot from the instructors and each other. Not to mention, it was a tax deductible trip and loads of fun!

Whether you take a solo retreat to the beach or the mountains, or participate in a group retreat, the focused writing time will allow you to hammer out a major portion of your book.

Outline
How-To Steps

Let's say you want to write a book that teaches a specific skill, concept, or strategy. This is what we would call a how-to book. This style of book is often formatted in steps.

Here are five steps to create a how-to book:

Step 1

Choose the strategy, concept, or skill you want to teach.

Step 2

Outline all the possible steps to implementing the strategy or concept, or developing the skill.

Step 3

Choose one step and write out, in detail, how to accomplish that step.

Step 4

Add to that step any general information your readers may need. For example, you may want to share pros and cons, helpful hints, or useful resources.

Step 5

Once you have written about each step, put them in sequential order. You have your finished manuscript! You can format the manuscript so that each chapter is a step (i.e., "Step 1" instead of "Chapter 1"), or you can eliminate the word *step* and simply state the action (e.g., Make An Outline or Define Each Step) as a title to begin each chapter.

How-to and step-by-step books are relatively easy to sell because the information is broken down in a concise, easy-to-digest format. Writing (or reading) this type of book can be excellent for anyone in a specialized trade such as organizing, interior decorating, plumbing, etc.

Answer the Question

Do you get asked the same questions over and over by different people? You may be able to answer those questions without thinking twice. Instead of simply giving a verbal response, carry a notebook with you and jot down questions after you answer them. If you come up with a great answer, write it down as well.

When you sit down to work on your book, pull out your notebook and begin answering those questions in more detail. Think about the Frequently Asked Questions pages you see on websites. Some of the answers on those pages are short, others are lengthy. Be as descriptive as necessary to make your answer clear to someone who knows absolutely nothing about the topic.

Remember that on a scale of one to ten, your knowledge on the topic you're writing about may fall anywhere between nine and fifteen. However, the average person's knowledge only falls around a two or three at best. Write for the two- or three-level readers, and you will probably be commended on how easy your information is to understand. Write at a level five or up, and you may end up with a bunch of frustrated, confused readers who give you poor reviews. You can always come out with an "advanced" book on the topic for readers who are more knowledgeable on the subject.

Take your collection of answers to a ghostwriter to fill in the gaps, or you can self-edit and fill in those gaps yourself. Gaps could be resources, tools, or additional information that helps clarify a particular point. Add transitions and make the answers flow together in one cohesive book.

If you answer enough questions about your field, industry, or a specific topic, you will have plenty of material for a book.

Fifteen Minutes a Day

Rome was not built in a day, neither are most books. Books are huge projects, and the primary reason they do not get written is lack of time.

As with any large project, it takes time to write a book. It also requires that you develop a habit of writing. It takes twenty-one days of consistent behavior to form a habit. So whether you blog, write a few paragraphs in your book project, outline a character's profile, write an article, or do some research for your book, make time to write or perform a writing-related activity every day.

Set aside a block of fifteen minutes each day and commit to writing. Make writing something you do automatically. You wouldn't think of skipping brushing your teeth in the morning; develop that same commitment to writing. Eventually, that short, fifteen minutes a day may turn into thirty, then sixty, then before you know it you will have spent several hours writing. Write consistently, and soon your book will become a reality.

Co-Author

If writing the entire book is too daunting a task, consider partnering with someone who has a complementary business or idea and can split the writing workload. This is frequently done in fiction genres where one person develops the idea and does the research while the other person writes the content.

Writing with someone else can speed the process because you're each doing half the work. It also helps to have another person to brainstorm with, help handle the research responsibilities, and lend new ideas.

The only caveat to consider is how well you and your co-author work together. Make sure your personality styles are compatible *before* getting into a large book project. Writing a book together is like being married for several months or even years. It can be stressful; you will get on each other's nerves. Be gracious and encouraging to each other. And, don't get so attached to your own ideas you are unwilling to consider your co-author's ideas.

Co-authoring gives you both the credibility you desire and often makes for stronger writing. You also have twice the sales team when it comes to marketing the book. In many authors' and publishers' eyes, this option is a win-win-win.

10

Compiled Blog Posts

If you have written steadily on a blog for a year or so, you probably have a ton of information that can be compiled into book format. Much like articles, blog posts can be placed into book form relatively easily. This method of compiled writing works for fiction, poetry, and non-fiction.

Here are some steps to compile your blog post information:

Step 1

Start reading. You may not want to publish your very early blog posts, but who knows? You could have some great material from way back then. Pull everything up and start reading.

Step 2

Copy/Paste. If you come across something that looks good, copy and paste it into a word processing program document. Remember to copy and paste the title there, too.

Step 3

Once you have copied and pasted everything you want in your book, check the length and begin organizing the content. If your book is a collection of poetry or short stories, you may not care about the order. If it is non-fiction, you may want to group it by topic.

Step 4

Hire a developmental editor. Unless your book is a collection of tips and strategies (like this book), you will want a developmental editor to help make the content flow. You originally wrote the book as individual blog posts that can stand alone. Now you need to link them all together. If you're like me and want your book to be the best it can be, a developmental editor is a must even for this style of book. My personal recommendation for developmental editing is Erin Casey at www.erin-casey.com.

Blogging is a great way to build your author platform and create publicity; it also gets you in the habit of writing and helps you master your skills. If your goal is to write a book, blog with that purpose in mind. A clear focus from the beginning will cut down on the amount of editing required later.

Co-Author with a Ghostwriter

As discussed on Way 9, co-authoring a book is a great way to produce a book. Alternatively, you can co-author with a ghostwriter, which means your name would appear alone on the book.

You still do half the work, whether in research and development, outlining chapters, or actual writing. The ghostwriter then takes your research, outlines, and any material you have written and expands on it to create the final book.

In the end, your name and credibility are attached to the book, and the ghostwriter is a silent partner. It is up to you if you want to add "with [Ghostwriter's Name Here]" under your byline on the cover. Some ghostwriters now require their names to go on the book under yours. For instance, if I used a ghostwriter for this book the author name on the front may read, "Kristen Eckstein, with Joe Schmoe." This gives the ghostwriter some exposure for writing, but it also shows how you had help writing the book.

Co-authoring with a ghostwriter can be very costly. However, it is a fantastic solution for busy people who want the instant credibility of being a published author, but don't have the time or the skill to write a book.

Part 2

Ways to Get Published

12

Paid-For Anthology

Any time your work is published in a book alongside other experts or authors, the piece is considered an *anthology*. You may, for example, write an article or chapter that is combined with others' work to create a larger book. Or you may write a chapter of a book for an industry association or a peer group on a specific topic such as "women in business."

An anthology can be a great way to get started in the book publishing industry. Here are a few pros and cons to this method of publication.

Pro #1

You usually only need to write one chapter. Depending on the anthology guidelines, the chapter can even be a long article you have already written. It doesn't need to take that long to complete.

Pro #2

The fact that your chapter is placed next to others who are considered experts in their fields will boost your credibility factor. This credibility by association can be a great perk if you are new to your field or industry. Positioning yourself alongside respected and well-known experts helps level the playing field.

Pro #3

Some anthology organizers will allow you to purchase a customized cover. If the cover features you with a few well-known experts, your credibility factor increases.

Con #1

Cost. The funding for these anthologies often comes from the authors; and it is not cheap. You can expect to pay anywhere from $400 to

$4,000 to be placed in the book, and there is usually a minimum book purchase required. If the anthology organizers plan to do any marketing for the book, you can expect to help pay for that as well.

Con #2

If you do not opt for a customized cover, the cover is either generic or the faces on the cover are all the "bigger" experts, not you. Additionally, most cover designs for these books are amateur at best.

Con #3

Though it does give you credibility to be placed with other experts, the downfall is that most people who understand how anthologies work know you paid for that position. This can potentially do as much harm as good.

Con #4

If your goal is to write a book specific to your industry, these generalized books may not be the best route to take. Nothing says, "I'm an expert" quite like a book with only your name on the cover and your content inside.

If you are interested in an anthology-type book that truly places you as the expert on the cover, is professionally edited and designed, has more financial investment from the publisher than from you, and can contribute significantly to back-of-the-room sales and additional income, check out 3Voices.com.

WAY 13

PDF eBook

PDF eBooks are very popular among small-business owners. A non-fiction eBook that is not also in print form typically runs about thirty pages. It is a very quick way to get your writing out there and call yourself an author.

However, many people do not want to pay for a thirty-page eBook. If you are willing to use the eBook as a freebie to get leads on your website, by all means choose this route.

Keep in mind that although an eBook can lend a level of credibility, it in no way replaces a print book. A print book of at least 120 pages speaks volumes about your expertise.

Another thing to be aware of when it comes to a PDF eBook is the fact that it is easily shared with others. A good graphic designer will have the ability to set security permissions on a PDF to disable printing or copying. However, if your eBook is simply a downloadable PDF, it is a file that can be shared by and with anyone. This is another reason to keep this style of publishing reserved for free offers.

That being said, this method is a great way to publish a book that can be sold as a low-dollar item, or use it as an "ethical bribe" for people to opt-in to your email list.

14

Contests

There are thousands of national and international writing contests, and many of them offer publication as part of the prize. Whether it is a short story contest that publishes the winner in a magazine, or a contest that submits the winning manuscript to a major agent, or one that offers to include the winner in an anthology for a vanity publisher, contests are one way to gain recognition for your writing and get published.

Here are some things to be aware of when entering contests:

The entry fee

Almost all contests have an entry fee. Most contests are created to be fundraisers for the organization. Or, entry fees may be used to front the money for prizes. Either way, find out whether the entry fee is per story, per poem, per article, or per group of works. Make sure you do the math and can afford entering—especially if you are considering entering multiple contests at once.

The publication requirements

Some contests will accept previously published material, but most require that the material is unpublished anywhere, including on your blog. Some contests will not accept material you have submitted to other contests. Research the requirements thoroughly before submitting your work.

Know your judges

Find out who the judges of the contest are and research their likes and dislikes. Remember that judges are looking for any excuse to *remove* your entry, not a reason to keep it. By knowing your judges, you can craft a piece they might enjoy, and give them a reason to keep your entry out of the trash pile.

Overall, contests can be an excellent way to get published and give you a feather in your hat of credibility. There is nothing like being able to say you are an award-winning author!

WAY 15

Vanity Publishing

Vanity publishing comes in many different forms. The two most common are:

Pay Now, Pay Later

One variation of vanity publishing is when you hire (a.k.a. pay) a company to publish your book. The company also takes a percentage of the profits of any book sold and pays you royalties.

"Free" Now, Pay a Lot More Later

Alternatively, a vanity publisher may agree to print your book for free, but will take full control of pricing and distribution, often pricing your book out of market range. This is to make up for the initial price tag of "free" and give the vanity publisher a large profit off every book sold.

In short, vanity is a good option for books that have an extremely small audience, such as poetry or memoire. It can be an inexpensive way to get a book done quickly.

However, you get what you pay for. Most companies provide little to no editing, create your book cover and interior with templates (which can make your book look like part of another person's series), and offer marketing support at high fees. In addition, vanity publishers slap their name (and reputation) on your book, which can greatly limit your sales potential at brick-and-mortar stores.

Vanity publishers also rarely meet the three criteria to get into bookstores: price point, return-ability, and wholesale discount.

My perception is that the vanity publishing industry is out to make a quick buck on poor-quality books. And they frequently cause authors un-necessary grief. These companies do not usually call themselves "vanity" due to the stigma of that term. Instead they try to mask themselves as other publishers, such as "self-publishing service provider" or "subsidy" or even stealing other proper terms such as "co-publishing," "self-publishing support" and even "indie."

If you choose a "paid-for publisher" to publish your book, do your research before signing a contract. Many vanity companies have been involved in lawsuits and class-action suits. Some have even had to change their business names as a result of legal action. They are notorious for not paying royalties, and for changing pricing on books whenever they want to whatever they see fit—without consulting the author.

If you plan to only write one poetry book, memoire, or one book of short stories, vanity may be a good option for you. But if you intend to write non-fiction, epic or fantasy fiction, or more than one book, vanity is probably not a good option.

Co-Publishing

Traditional publishers are suffering, so they have come up with a form of "vanity" publishing to help increase their bottom lines. This new co-publishing option can help authors increase their potential for moving into the company's traditional publishing division.

Depending on your goals, co-publishing with a traditional house is not a bad option. Most major publishing houses that offer the co-publishing option screen manuscripts and are not out to make a quick dollar off of the author. Most of them legitimately want to gauge a new author's potential before signing a traditional book deal. The publisher may even put the strength of their marketing and distribution behind the book. If the book sells well, the publisher may decide to move the title into its traditional line.

The primary downfall to this type of publishing is the price tag. It can be very expensive to co-publish, as the author still fronts the cost as they would in vanity or self-publishing. Also, their rights may not be kept in full. It is always a good practice to thoroughly read the contract and understand exactly what you are getting your-self into. You may also want to have an agent represent you and review the contracts, even in a co-publishing scenario.

Some publishing houses have chosen to part-ner with major vanity publishing companies for the development of this option. This is an unfor-tunate practice that causes strife to the author as you are now subject to the vanity company's reputation and practices, not the traditional publisher.

Do your research, know what you are getting into, and have clear goals and reasons for choos-ing this publishing route. It can be a win-win for both author and publisher, but it can also be a major win-lose (publisher wins, you lose).

eBook Publishing

As mentioned in Way 13, a PDF eBook (about 30 pages) is an excellent way to quickly become an author. You can also create your book as you would a print book, but have it distributed in eBook format.

An eBook has the same cost of development as a print book, including editing, design, typesetting, etc., but its production costs are much lower. In fact, other than the required discount to online retailers, an eBook costs nothing to produce.

You can write a book, distribute it quickly and easily as an eBook, and have the price point lower than a print book so you sell more copies.

One downfall to the eBook craze is it still does not give you the same credibility as a print book. That added cost of paper, plus the feel of a "real" book in your hands, is still a major selling point. If your goal is to get published quickly and somewhat easily, eBooks are for you. But if your goal is to establish credibility, have a nice promotional item, or increase the cost of workshops and seminars with a free copy of your book as a bonus, then publishing it only as an eBook is not for you.

Another downfall to eBooks is an issue with various eBook retailers. Ingram Digital, the main wholesaler/distributor of eBooks, only issues Adobe Digital Editions format. In an effort to force publishers to use new technology, major eBook retailers such as Amazon.com refuse to recognize the longtime standard Adobe eBook format, or sell it. But the technology is flawed. I recently downloaded current, traditionally published titles to my Kindle and found that almost every page had typos, words stuck on other words, random spacing or hyphens breaking words apart, etc., which made it frustrating and difficult to read.

The tried-and-true Adobe eBook format (readable by any eBook reader, including the Kindle) retains all the formatting of the original book, eliminating this problem. Unfortunately for authors, the Kindle Store on Amazon.com has chosen to stop selling Adobe eBooks. That means additional formatting to "pretty up" the interior of your book can cost a small fortune— with the only benefit being a listing in the Kindle Store. For more on this discussion, check out my blog post at: www.KristenEckstein. com/2011/02/the-kindle-store-problem.

Since the setup and creation of the Adobe eBook format is the same as a print book, my question is, why not do both and have the best of both the print and online worlds? Then if you wish to sell the book in the Kindle Store, the option is always available to have it re-formatted to fit their guidelines.

18

Critique-Group Anthology

If you are a member of a writing organization, you may have the opportunity to be published in an anthology created by that organization's critique group. The Writer's Group of the Triad (TriadWriters.org), a writer's group in Greensboro, North Carolina, has produced a number these anthologies. Many authors published in this group's anthologies have gone on to become well-known authors.

Critique groups give you the ability to create stronger pieces and you don't have to write the entire book yourself. You get your work published faster, better, and benefit from the support and name recognition of a larger organization. A critique-group anthology is an excellent way to publish fiction, short stories, children's work, poetry, and creative non-fiction.

This type of anthology is a fantastic way to build your résumé, get exposure, and support your local critique groups all at the same time.

Traditional Publishing

Traditional publishing is still the mainstay in the industry. Traditional publishing houses control the major distribution channels to bookstore outlets. And there's no denying the fact that authors receive an ego boost from having a "big name" on their books. But, there are pros and cons to traditional publishing.

Pro #1

The ego boost. Having a big publisher backing your work strokes your ego.

Pro #2

Distribution. Though independently published books have access to the same distributors, traditional publishers still have the power to get a book on massive numbers of bookstore shelves at the same time. Most publishers guarantee the book to be on the shelf for three months, and some pay for premium placement in the stores—on end caps or in the front of the store—to feature hot authors and best-selling books.

Pro #3

The advance. Most first-time fiction authors can expect an advance of up to $5,000. Non-fiction books currently average around $1,000 for *first-time* authors. This can be helpful in funding your marketing budget for the book.

Con #1

Timing. Traditional publishing can now take as little as eighteen months from acceptance to completed book. But the time spent securing an agent and selling your book to the publisher, combined with the actual publication and production time still adds up to anywhere from three to five years.

Con #2

Distribution. Yes, publishing houses guarantee your book will stay on the shelf for three months. But unless your book becomes a bestseller during that timeframe, it is removed from the shelf, sold in the clearance or discount section, and made a "backlist" title. You do not have the power to keep the book on the shelf longer.

Con #3

Marketing. If you are a first-time author, you are responsible for all your own marketing. Sometimes your contract will require you to use your entire advance on marketing, and you may even be required to hire a PR firm your publisher recommends. A good PR firm will cost over $1,000 per month and most demand a six-month minimum contract. I'll let you do the math on how long your advance will last.

You have to decide for yourself if the traditional route is best for your goals for your book. If you are already a successful author or have a large platform, you may be able to get a great traditional book deal. And it is not bad to have that publisher name to boost your credibility even further.

Indie Publishing

Some vanity companies call themselves indie publishers nowadays; be careful. Please remember the definitions of a vanity publisher in Way 15. Indie is short for "independent" and means just that. You, the author, are in charge of everything from finding an editor and book designer, to setting up an account with a printer and then of course, marketing.

Do not be fooled by vanity publishers who claim successful books have been "self-published" and that by hiring them to publish your book you can achieve the same success. The truth is vanity and indie are both forms of self-publishing because the author is paying the up-front cost of the book's production. But the successful self-published books vanity publishers often refer to—*The One Minute Manager, The Christmas Box, Chicken Soup for the Soul, The Shack, Eragon*—were strictly *indie* published. The author's (or the author's company's) name is on the back of the book—not some vanity publishing company's name. (Visit IamPublished.com for a done-for-you indie publishing system that combines the ease of vanity with the control and benefits of indie.)

There is only one major con to indie publishing and several pros:

Con

Indie is true self-publishing, so you as the author must front the total cost to bring your book to market. That cost can vary greatly depending on your skills and the people you know who can help you. It can range from as little as $400, to as high as $7,000 or more.

Pro #1

With indie publishing, you only have your reputation to worry about, not that of another company.

Pro #2

You retain full control over every aspect, including distribution.

Pro #3:

The publication timeline can be as short as one month to bring your book to market. And you have control over whether or not you want to sell your book to a traditional publisher down the road. Which brings us to Way 21 . . .

21

Two-Track Publishing

You can go through the publication process as an indie-publisher and secure an agent to represent your book to traditional publishers at the *same exact time*. This option allows you to release your book quickly and begin building a sales record through the indie process—giving an agent (or you) ammunition to fight for a higher advance and higher royalties.

You can choose to sell your current title to a traditional publisher, or give them rights to a future book. Three of my indie-publishing consulting clients are currently under contract with major traditional publishers. Two are writing new books for the publishers and one sold her current book to a traditional house. One of those authors was offered a non-fiction advance for her new book five times the size of the average first-time author advance.

You may be required to change or increase your book's content if you choose to sell your current title to a traditional publisher, so sometimes writing a new book is a better choice. Plus any books sold with the power of that traditional team will drive sales toward your indie-published book that nets you 100 percent of the profits.

In my opinion, Two-Track Publishing is the best way to go. Not only do you get the possibility of a higher advance, higher royalties, and that traditional name on your book, but you retain the control and benefits indie publishers enjoy.

Conclusion

I hope your brain is whirring with many new ideas gleaned from reading this little book. Now that you have *21 Ways to Write and Publish Your Non-Fiction Book* in-hand, it's time to start writing! No excuses—go write, now!

About the Author

Kristen Eckstein has earned the title "The Ultimate Book Coach" from her many clients.

She entered the world of business at six years old selling homemade "pet" rocks, experienced the success and failure of several businesses before entering High School, started her first IRS-reportable business in college and earned her Bachelor of Fine Art degree in 2002. Her work has been published in books, magazines, on greeting cards, and classroom supplies. She currently serves as Executive Producer for Imagine! Studios, an art and media production company co-founded with her husband Joe and she eats chocolate for breakfast.

She has been in the "book sucking" business since 2003 and has a passion for indie publishing, which is in her humble opinion the sweetest form of publishing that exists on planet Earth. (She calls it "white chocolate publishing.")

She is very proud of her *I am Published!*™ program graduates, including Bob The Teacher Jenkins, Felicia Slattery, Paul Evans, Lindy Clark, Loretta Lutman, Phil Simon, Dr. "Mommy" Daisy Sutherland, and more!

Her favorite thing in the world is to see YOU hug your book for the very first time!

That is, next to chocolate for breakfast.

To learn more about Kristen, visit
UltimateBookCoach.com.

For more information on how to finish your book (or get started!), visit FinishTheBook.com.

And for the "sweetest" done-for-you indie publishing system in the world, visit IamPublished.com.

She looks forward to hearing from you!

You can write a book in 3 1/2 days!

Get **FREE** instant access to my training video and watch and listen as I share my secrets for finishing your book in 3 1/2 days!

Rebecca Morus I just listened to your free training video on "Write Your Book in 3.5 days! I was thrilled with the insightful information you provided. Although, I have not ventured into writing books- I've made many attempts to write scripts. You provided a "real world" instructions on how to actually finish those ideas swarming in my head! I'll definitely be able to use this on my next project!

42 minutes ago · Like

Bethany Williams Thank you for sharing this. I took some wonderful tips from this video. And the fact that it is FREE is extremely generous. Sharing any information about writing for FREE is quite a gift. I can't thank you enough! Also, I am inspired to buckle down and focus. A great kick in the pants. Just what I needed today. =)

6 hours ago · Unlike · 👍 1 person

WriteMyBookIn3Days.com

It's time for you to...

FINISH
the Book!™
www.finishthebook.com

What's stopping you from
finishing YOUR book?

Are you a master procrastinator who takes time for everyone and everything except writing?

Do you suffer from the most common of all writers' woes – writer's block?

Are you caught in an endless battle with your internal editor, convinced your prose is never "good" enough?

Have you convinced yourself that you're simply too busy to commit to writing now? Maybe you'll get around to it later…

Yes, YOU Can Accomplish Something
Most People Only Dream Of!

I've been where you are, and I know you probably want to:

Say good-bye to that sick feeling that you're just not good enough to write a book,

End the sense of being overwhelmed, and turn your project into a reasonable to-do list you can actually accomplish,

And... Finally have a finished manuscript to show in answer to the endless question, "Is your book done yet?"

Your time has come.

FinishTheBook.com

Are you ready to say...

I am
Published!™
www.iampublished.com

Have you started researching your publishing options, but don't know an ISBN from an ATM?

Do you know how to find a good copyeditor?

Do you wish your book would be done for you?

Are you concerned about giving up your distribution and repurposing rights?

If you answered, "Yes" to any of the above, you are a fantastic candidate for the Ghost Publishing program, *I am Published!*™.

Besides having 100% control over your project, you will:

Get published in your name without the hassle of handling everything yourself,

Have NO association with a vanity publishing company (or their reputation),

Keep 100% of the profits of every book sold, (Who needs royalties?)

Meet the criteria to be stocked in bookstores,

Keep the option open to negotiate with a traditional publisher,

Avoid "paying later" with every book you sell,

And... Keep all your rights, *including* distribution and repurposing rights.

Don't wait. Join these successful authors today!

IamPublished.com

You've written. You're published. Now it's time to...

Market My Book!™
www.marketmybooknow.com

in Less than One Hour!

You've just written or published a must-read, literary masterpiece that is truly "un-put-downable," a book that will help businesses grow enough to add thousands of jobs to the economy...

But how do you get it in front of people to purchase and read?

If you are like many authors, you know there are hundreds of ways to market your book online and off. The problem is you don't know where to start. And, there is no getting around having a solid book marketing plan in place. It doesn't even matter if you decide to go the traditional book publishing route; you still need to know how to create a marketing plan, because it's now part of your book proposal to publishers. They will require it.

The *Market My Book!*™ program will show you how to create a 4-Month Marketing Plan lickety split!

When you finish this program, you'll know:

The different forms of marketing and how to leverage them to gain publicity,

How to leverage Social Media: Twitter, Facebook, LinkedIn, YouTube and more,

Unique ways to package your book to stand out and make an impression,

How to do pay-per-click the right way,

The basics behind online strategy and internet marketing,

And much, much more…